Definitely a book that is entering the world at a time when it is needed the most, MOJO FOR SALE by Katandra Jackson Nunnally offers you the keys to your freedom and the opportunity to realize your own endless possibilities.

~Cyrus A. Webb, Conversations Magazine

Mojo For Sale

The Art of Encouraging One's Self

By Katandra Jackson Nunnally

FreedomInk

PO Box 1093 Reidsville Georgia 30453

Copyright 2014

by Katandra Jackson Nunnally

Cover design by Elaina Lee.

Page layout by FreedomInk Publishing.

Final edit by Katandra Jackson Nunnally.

ISBN 978-0-9896786-1-2

Printed in the United States of America

http://www.freedomink365.com

There are some pretty amazing full length novels available at FreedomInk Publishing. You should totally check them out!

'Woman on Fire' by Trinette Collier

'Anybody's Somebody' by Phoenix

'Life & Love Through My Eyes'
by Ramona Jones

'The Lady, Niobe' by Kenny L. Mitchell

'Jareth, First Lord' by Mellie Miller

Other books by Katandra Shanel Jackson...

The Diary of A Bride To Be Books 1, 2 & 3

Angel Eyes: A Collective Memoir of Child
Sexual Abuse

A Room Of Her Own

Carnal Sobriety

Vantage Points

ACKNOWLEDGEMENTS

Cyrus Webb, you & every endeavor that you are a part of is pretty darn amazing. You have erected a platform for individuals with special talents to share. Rather they be musically inclined, artistic or gifted writers. No matter the phase they are in, be it established or emerging… You've welcomed each and made every guest feel right at home! I have watched you work tirelessly to present these individuals to the World! On behalf of FreedomInk, myself the CEO & the Authors, we thank you. Keep those Conversations flowin'!

David Avery, the go to guy if anyone has questions pertaining Tattnall County & my hometown, Reidsville Georgia! Thanks for keeping your ear to the ground and always knowing what's going on and for providing the opportunity to be seen & heard where so many others would never have dared. At the end of the day, it's all about the books! Let's get this community reading. The World begins at my own backdoor!

DEDICATION

As an Author, I biasedly feel that every book I compose should be dedicated either to a very specific audience of readers or to the nuclear family. Since this book was written to be presented & accepted by a pretty universal readership, I suppose I'll be dedicating it to the nuclear family. You know, that special set of individuals who brave to reside in a home with a writer. Where everything they say and do may just end up in a book.

I dedicate this book to my children, Jermaine Trevon, Kailyn Elise & Ashley Vanique Jackson, and my husband, Jeremy C. Nunnally. You guys and gals not only tolerate my strangeness, you welcome it, you nurture it, sometimes I swear y'all encourage it. For that I love you & dedicate this and every book to each of you!

SPECIAL THANKS

I'd like to extend a very special thank you to 5 very special individuals! My sister in law, Laura Johnson. A dear childhood friend, Maurice McNeal. My comrade in arms, Yvette Porter Moore. A friend whom I consider to be my Scorpio Twin, Ivory Coburn. And last but not least, my 5th Grade Language Arts Teacher, Andrea Ashford Levant!

I just want to go on the record and give a very public thanks. When the idea for this book impregnated itself in my psyche, I had no idea who I would turn to for advice. You 5 voluntarily agreed to be my soundboard. You were honest & quite frankly, extra opinionated. For that, I am forever grateful! Thank you.

Mojo

For

Sale

The Art of Encouraging One's Self

By Katandra Jackson Nunnally

FOREWORD

As a Mother, Wife, Daughter, Sister, TeeTee (super cool Aunt and Godmother), Author, Publisher, awesome, amazing, absolutely astounding, forever encouraging friend, I often find myself, an oasis of motivation & inspiration.

Too often I've found myself on the short end of the receiving stick. So instead of constantly casting my line into waters that have forgotten that sometimes I need a boost too, I've decided to dig in and create my own little wellspring of encouragement.

I've given it away, freely in adequate and absurd amounts. Now it's time I keep some for myself. However, I've decided to offer a small percentage of my mojo for sale! So here it is...

INTRODUCTION

The premise for this book planted itself deep in my heart & rapidly began to flourish. But how would I go about composing a book from just a thought? Sure the idea is a good one & the title is pretty clever if I may say so myself. But where to begin? How to start? What should be the content of this book? So I asked myself, "What encourages me?" Believe me, it's not as easy to answer as you might think.

"What encourages me?"

The first response that comes to mind, as I've been a parent for a very long time. At 34 years and 8 months young (with a newly turned 17 year old), honestly, I've been a parent for at least ½ of the life I've lived thus far. Okay... My children encourage me! What else? My mother, my step-father, my brothers, my family! These are all easy go to answers. But who & what beyond my immediate family & those individuals that reside in my innermost sanctum, encourages me? The silent response is unsettling! No wonder I've been feeling slightly jaded, quite upset. My Mojo is running low. The current level is dangerously close to a complete depletion. So instead of waiting for those around me to make a few deposits, I've decided to go in search for those things that will replenish my Mojo in all its splendor!

LETTER TO THE READER

Dear Reader,

'Mojo For Sale' is a compilation of some of the things that encourage me. Set to print & published for the World to see. The chapters are short as it is not my desire to hold you hostage here between the covers of this book. Oh no! I'd much rather give it to you straight, no chaser and send you confidently out into the World, on a mission to discover & reapply that which inspires, motivates and ultimately encourages you.

Some sources will reveal themselves easily and readily; you need not look far for these. Others however, may take some soul searching, some serious contemplation, in the very least, some deep thought. But fret not. By the time you reach the last chapter, I know that you'll feel confident in this search. The tools to gather encouragement from said sources reside in you. I implore you, enjoy the read and the journey!

SOURCES

FAMILY...

I know that family should all be the same. But for me, the members of my family reside on three very different plateaus.

I. There are those who've raised you & whom you grew up with. Parents, Guardians, Siblings.

II. There are those you've raised & watched grow up. Your children. In some cases, your siblings.

III. And then there is everyone else! Aunts, Uncles, cousins, grandparents...

Hopefully, prayerfully, your family like mine is a constant although sometimes forgotten source of encouragement. They are always there! Telling you what to do and what not to do. Offering their opinions & advice in such an interjecting manner, that it's almost always given when it's not needed... Allowing you to make your own decisions when you most need their butting in. Bickering. Arguing. Nagging. Getting on your nerves. But this guiding, this helping you grow up, that sense of this network of individuals that belong just to you, is always there.

I do understand that sometimes, the family that is your source of encouragement, may not always be genetically linked to you. That's okay. Adopted families that lovingly chose you and friends you've chosen with love whom occupy your innermost sanctum, they too are your family and are an amazing source of encouragement!

During this search to replenish my Mojo, I will honor my parents. I will forgive any hard feelings that have survived the years and linger still. I will pardon all and any indiscretions. I will honor my mother & my father as I give thanks for the beautiful conception which ultimately consummated in the wonderful works which is the creation of me! I'm glad for the encouraging source which is my family.

FRIENDS...

Friends... How many of us have them? There may not be an entourage at your every beck and call, but most of us can at least lay claim to a few whom they truly consider friends. Rather you have lots in common or a little, our friends like us because of who we are. Your friends like you because you are the only you that can be YOU! Did you get that? Friends don't question your quirks. They embrace them as they embrace you.

Friends don't shun you because of your differences. Sadly, but understandably, sometimes families do! Apple trees are supposed to bear apples. So if the branch that births you produces a grapefruit, well... The family may not take too kindly to the 'odd' one! It may seem a bit extreme, they may not even know that they've been doing it, but sometimes, just sometimes, our families cast us out as the 'Black Sheep'. But never our friends. In this simple act of unconditional acceptance, our friends give us the courage to be ourselves. This fanning of that inner sense of strength is all encompassing and extremely encouraging!

I will give thanks to the Universe for sending those special individuals into my life. Thank you for their never shunning kindness. Thank you for their sympathetic understanding. Thank you for their non-judgmental acceptance. Thank you for their constant approval. These super beings just get it. They shall from henceforth and forevermore be called 'friend'. Our friends are an amazing source of encouragement!

FOES

Don't take the word too literally. I'm not suggesting we go around harboring hate in our hearts. No malice, please! Only love & peace... Ideally in an absolute perfect World. But by no means am I so naïve as to believe that we live in such a utopic place! I can 'see' the hate. So much animosity. So much energy wasted. There are those that pray against you and truly wish for you to meet your demise. There are those in our lives who'd rather not acknowledge your success. An old classmate. A friend or a fried of a friend whom you sensed never liked you. A family member... It can happen.

No I'm not telling you these things to discourage you. The purpose in this chapter is to embolden you in the search for the silver lining in that very dark cloud. There is always a silver lining! If only our foes knew that their ill thoughts and negative feelings have the potential to add fuel to the fire, in a positive way. They are not the only driving force, but c'mon... You gotta admit, there's something rather delicious in making it in spite of the naysayers!

I won't give constant thought to my foes. I will accept the fact that more than likely they do exist. Seen and unseen. I will not allow the stench of ill wishes to reign over my parade. I will be encouraged by those who are standing in line, waiting ever so patiently to see me fail. I will not forget to acknowledge the bumps along the way. They make for a much more interesting ride. My foes are an unexpected source of encouragement.

CHILDREN

If you're a parent, I know what you're thinking! But aren't these particular creatures, miniature extensions of ourselves? Therefore placing them in the category 'Family'. With that I bid thee, touché. But of course your children are your family. But they are such special beings, that I truly did feel that they deserved their own chapter. Also, for those reading who may not be parents but whom would still like to receive from the Universe, the encouragement that only a child could give… Keep reading!

You don't have to be a parent. There's an old African Proverb that states, 'It takes a Village to raise a child.' This is so very true. Every adult a child encounters has the opportunity to influence that child. It's only natural, that if you're paying attention, if you're truly attuned to the environment surrounding you, the children that you encounter will influence you too!

Filled with innocent glee & wonder! Children are at that remarkable stage in life when they are most fearless! They still have the audacity to be bold, to be adventurous and dare I say it... Children are not afraid to dream! Oh, imagine the World we'd inhabit if we all saw life & lived wholeheartedly through a child's eyes.

I will put aside my selfish grown up ways and become more like my inner child. Caring, compassionate, considerate, un-callous! I will achieve these things by mirroring the actions of my own children. They unknowingly encourage me by simply being. All the children of the World are an amazing source of encouragement.

COLLEAGUES

Be they Coworkers sitting adjacent in the office cubicle next to yours or Cyber Buds whom you interact with solely online, who just happen to be in the same profession as yourself, our Colleagues encourage us. There are two types of encouragement that our Colleagues offer.

I. Active Encouragement! You see your Colleagues working hard, striving to be their best and give their all. Further propelling their career, their company and their Coworkers. These are my favorite type of Colleagues! All one has to do is be in their midst. That 'Go Getter' attitude is most contagious.

II. Inactive Encouragement! Try as you might to avoid the 'Office Leper' but you just can't seem to escape their bubble. It bumps into you throughout the day. You just want to pop it… That bubble of absolute nothingness. This is the Colleague you can often find working hard to do the least. You can spot them from a mile away. Their nonchalant attitude is a perfect example of what not to do! There is all sorts of encouragement derived of the slacker! But beware! That 'Why Bother' attitude is also contagious.

I see them. Those who reside in my chosen profession. Coworkers and Cyber Buds. We share the same work interest. I will watch each type of Colleague, daily. The encouragement found in both active and inactive individuals, will not be in vain! Repeat after me... "I will strive to be the very best (insert your profession here) that I can be! The examples before me are like the fruit of an apple tree. I will choose carefully which to eat and which to leave. For either way, that which I consume, becomes me and that which I leave, further encourages me to be the best I can be."

PHYSICAL BITS

& PIECES

The World is comprised of an infinite culmination of physical bits & pieces. They are way too many to list within this short chapter. So instead of making an attempt to do the impossible, I'll simply take you on a make believe tour of my home! I'd have you to close your eyes but you may bump into walls.

Location: My humble abode.

Mission: Locate physical bits & pieces that invoke motivation and inspiration and in turn, provokes a euphoric sense of encouragement within me.

Actual items found on this make believe tour of my home that encourage me are as listed…

Elephants. Of every shape and size. Varying in material. Glass. Ceramic. Wood. Stainless Steel. The elephant is a beautiful creature in life. They are family oriented and depend on a Matriarch to lead and be the head of the family. This is very symbolic of the once upon a time, on again, off again, single parent home I've maintained throughout the course of my children's youth. The elephant encourages me to put my family first. That no matter what, a mother must do what a mother must do!

Globes and maps of the World. Another source of encouragement from the 'Physical Bits & Pieces' realm! These things remind me that no matter where I'm from, where I may be or the place it seems I'm heading, the World is a great big ol' place! There are millions with far worse problems than my own. Not to poke and prod at those who are metaphorically drowning, but let's face it… If you're reading this book, the chances are highly likely that you are in the very least, in the boat so to speak. What I'm saying is, don't get so down on yourself when you're going through a hard time. You ain't the only one! Aside from putting my minor issues into perspective, the globes and maps in my home remind me that even though I grew up in a town (Manassas Georgia) whose population has yet to progress beyond 200 via any given Census, the places my Passport can take me are far from that place. It's a very comforting thought.

Books! As an Author and Publisher, these physical bits & pieces are very direct sources of encouragement. By the hundreds, the books in my home encourage me to keep writing. In a sea of television, social media and cell phone games & apps, pursuing this literary dream often leaves me feeling like the little fish. But keep swimming I must. The books, they whisper to me to keep moving my pen and publishing books, no matter what! The waters may seem a little choppy at first, but there are smooth seas ahead.

Photographs of my family are cute, colored, sometimes sephia or black and white, visual mementos. They are always on display. Watching me from walls, mantles & desktops as I move through every day. Reminding me that, 'Hey, remember what you said about family encouraging you? Well, here we are… Go forth and be encouraged!'

Family heirlooms… There is one relic from my past that I of all people in my family, have inherited! It is my Great Grandmother Frankie's china cabinet. Over a century ago, it belonged to her. She passed it down to her daughter, my Grandmother Mertis, who left charge of it with my own Mother, Vernice. Now I must admit, acquiring this family heirloom came as quite a shock to me. You see I have the soul of a Gypsy. I get weary once I've been in a place too long. Still, my Mother saw enough stability in my wandering ways to put this beautiful piece of my past in my care! The very presence of this 4th Generation heirloom in my home encourages me.

Today I am glad that I needn't go farther than my own home to be encouraged. These physical bits & pieces totally rock the Universe of personal possessions and Worldly belongings! I'm so glad they are mine.

ALL THE WORDS

Verses. Quotes. Sayings. Poems...

We all have different interpretations preset in our minds for each of these encouraging things! When I hear the word 'Verse' I automatically think of the Bible. I'm not overly religious, but I do believe that all things, including every religion, are but pieces of a whole and there is only one Creator... But that's another chapter. Back to finding our Mojo!

When it comes to encouraging yourself, one must discover the verses, quotes, sayings and poems that work best for you! I wish you happy hunting on this particular leg of the journey! Deciding your favorites is only half the fun.

You can choose as many verses, quotes, sayings and poems as you'd like. There are a few of each that I call upon when I need a boost. The all-knowing power attached to these words seem to have some elasticity effect over me. No matter how ill the mood I may be in, reading or reciting the verses, quotes, sayings and poems that work for me, instantaneously encourage me to keep striving. There's still plenty of road left to travel and I intend to see every mile of it. All the words encourage me to spring back to life!

Verse: Psalm 1:3 reads, "That person is like a tree planted by streams of water, which yields its fruit in season and whose leaf does not wither—whatever they do prospers."

Quote: "Imperfection is beauty, madness is genius and it's better to be absolutely ridiculous than absolutely boring." ~Marilyn Monroe

Saying: The famous athletic wear brand, Nike, has a saying, "Just do it!"

Poem: 'Invictus' by William Ernest Henley. It's a classic. My favorite lines from that poem are:

> Beyond this place of wrath and tears
> Looms but the Horror of the shade,
> And yet the menace of the years
> Finds, and shall find, me unafraid.

All the words in all the World encourage me to keep writing, keep reading, keep being. So I will write. I will read. I will be. I will call upon those verses, quotes, sayings and poems that are the most profound to me. They will uplift me and I will be all the more glad for them! The complexity of a string of simple words is beyond measure.

What words encourage you?

AFFIRMATIONS

Webster's Dictionary defines Affirmations as 'a solemn and often public declaration of the truth or existence of something'. No, you don't have to go broadcasting your affirmation, it need only be public domain to your mind, body, soul and heart! A few years ago I was challenged by a friend to compose my own positive self-affirmation. It wasn't easy. The question of what to affirm, or declare, hung dark and luminous as a storm cloud overhead. This was gonna require some spirit delving! I've had some hard truths to accept in my life. I knew my affirmation could not be written without acknowledging those old hurts. But instead of disregarding that ancient pain, I chose instead to build my affirmation from the scars that most spend their whole lives covering up… Here I share my positive self-affirmation with you in hopes that you will be encouraged to do some self-assessing and determine that you are worthy of an awesome life. Your affirmation will remind you of the public declaration of the truth which is YOU (ARE) and the existence of something GREAT!

My Daily Affirmation

By: Katandra Shanel Jackson

I am strong. A force to be reckoned with.
I am a Survivor.

I am smart. Seeking truth beyond knowledge.
I am a student.

I am sexy. But just because I possess this sassy
trait, does not mean it defines me.
I am more than my body.

I am steadfast. Diligent in my efforts, giving
210% at all time. What I put forth, I shall
receive 10 fold. I am the Sower.

Above all these things, yet intricately entwined,
I know that the beauty which exudes me,
radiates from within and I am
MAGNIFICENT!!

Now it's your turn! What will you affirm? I
challenge you to write it and recite it… Daily.
Say it till you believe it!

Today I affirm that I am beautifully human and that means that I am not without flaws. But I refuse to allow life's obstacles to dull my brilliance. I will repeat daily, this affirmation that I have composed and publicly declared to my heart to be the truth. Positive self-affirmations, especially when recited daily and whole heartedly believed, will encourage me! The affirmation that I am great is received.

I challenge you to write your own Affirmation!

MANTRAS

& MEDITATION

Mantras & Meditations are not created equal. However, both serve as a very powerful Mojo replenisher! Let's discover the difference in the two and apply them immediately! Well, not too immediately. It takes some practice to introduce mantras and meditation to your life. If you're anything like me, your days are uber busy. Business is synonymous with chaos and chaos is loud! If you're assuming that this source of encouragement requires a sense of serenity, from my understanding, you're right!

Defining a word: "Mantra" (Sanskrit मंत्र) means a sacred utterance, numinous sound, or a syllable, word, phonemes, or group of words believed by some to have psychological and spiritual power. Mantra may or may not be syntactic or have literal meaning; the spiritual value of mantra comes when it is audible, visible, or present in thought. {Wikipedia}

"Meditation" is a practice in which an individual trains the mind or induces a mode of consciousness, either to realize some benefit or as an end in itself. {Wikipedia}

Both of these definitions are verbatim per Wikipedia {8_18_14}. My overall take on it all, as these two simple words hold a vast amount of weight is this. Mantras are something you repeat to yourself during meditation. Or perhaps meditation is a way to channel mantras. The two are separate entities but they seem to go hand in hand. When it comes to seeking out and securing the sources that will aid in the replenishment of your mojo, I highly recommend researching and learning as much as you can about mantras and meditation.

Today, I wholeheartedly acknowledge that anything that brings me to a plane of spiritual awareness and higher consciousness, is certainly worth my pursuit! Enlightened, I am encouraged.

HIGHER POWER

There are a lot of different religions in the World. Most of which each believe in a Higher Power. Be it Gods and Goddesses, Deities, graven images, Idols, Prophets, a multitude of Divinities, one God or purely the belief that there is a Higher Power that oversees & protects all things! I usually claim to be more of a spiritual being. Jeans and tee, sandals and kinky braids, free spirit, one love kinda gal… That's me! I'm still working my way up to this realm of religion. But my lack to lay stake with any one denomination, does not mean I don't concede a Higher Power. I do. I refer to this Higher Power as The Most High.

I was not raised in a religious home environment. It wasn't until my teenage years when I would be introduced to Bible Study. We had a very special Teacher that not only taught from the 'good book', he also challenged his pupils. He'd tell us after every Sunday School session, "Don't take my word for it. Go out and find out for yourself!" It was with this prompting that I would set out upon a quest that has yet to yield its sweetest fruits, but the seed has been planted.

My belief lie heavily in The Story of Babel. I sincerely believe that every aspect that divides us as a human being (language, ethnicity, beliefs, religion) was long ago, all a part of the same and that this theory can be tracked back to this ancient tale! To believe that there is something in me that is a part of all things that was created by a Higher Power, is an amazing feeling. One like none other in fact. With this feeling surging through every part of myself, my mojo is strengthened even more!

On this mission to get my mojo back, I will seek thee that made me! He that created me shall not fail me. He slumbers not nor sleeps. He is tireless in his attempts to take care of me. And in lieu of the restlessness of The Most High, I shall not grow weary on this journey. My mojo will be restored!

UNIVERSE

Such a sad thing to admit, but it seems that there will always be some degree of madness in the World. Even still, beyond every irrational act, I have this all-consuming thought. I'm a proud inhabitant of the Universe. She belongs to me, and I to her. It is my duty to make her proud. This thought further leads me to believe that I have a responsibility to be the best version of me that I can be… The Universe is my birthright. Every generation born will inherit her. She is overflowing with numerous sources and a wide array of resources, each readily available and quite at your dispose. Aching to be recycled. Put into you so that you can put back into the Universe, all that mojo entails. The inspiration, the motivation, the encouragement…. The knowledge, the beauty, the kindness.

If not wielded properly, the mojo restorative sources of the Universe, can be detrimental. Instead when seeking out this cradle which swaddles your birthright, let's commit to paying it forward. That which we take we will replace. The Universe is a boundless, limitless source of encouragement. Once firmly within our grasp, lets choose to use it wisely.

Today I attest that I am one with the Universe. Every thing that I need can be found at her feet. I am the Harvester. I will gather these things. I will take only that which is needed. My mojo will be steadily replenished! With access to this source that cannot be denied, I give thanks to the Universe for that which is mine. It shall be given freely to those that I encounter if they wish to unlock this source. Isn't that after all, what this journey all about?

ME

If for some very odd reason, you can't seem to locate a valid, relevant, accessible source of replenishment on this quest to augment your mojo, I suggest you to take a good, long, hard look in the mirror. See that person staring back at you? You know the one! Always a beacon of light. Others gravitate to you for inspiration, motivation and encouragement! You are overflowing with joy that anyone would think so highly as to trust you to add to their mojo from your own reserves. So then what makes you doubt that there will be none leftover for you?

There are countless animals that call this planet home. Of them, the strangest in my opinion are those that have the ability to regenerate limb simply by being alive! Unless you're reading this book from some un-living World, you're alive and prayerfully well. Hopefully by now you can see where I'm going! By simply being alive, there is a source nearby that you don't have to travel far to find. It's breathing, bleeding, heart beating... YOU! If you're a Nurturer, like me, it's easy to give, give, give till your mojo is all gone! And being the classic Nurturer, you could never ask for even a small portion of that encouragement in return. You'll give all of you until there is nothing left. But fret not Seekers. Your mojo is just as much an extension of you as any appendage!

Believe in that restorative, regenerative ability. Breathe life into your mojo and know that it deserves to be replenished. Have faith that if you will it, it will be so!

Living is no simple thing. It's complex and filled with delicate, detailed intricacies that cease to amaze. There is a great big ol' World out there, teeming with people. Each of us connected by some common thread. Ethnicity, language, background, belief, family life, career, education, talents-skills-hobbies. The things that bind us are far too many to list. Even still, despite these things, I am the only ME!

DISCOVER
YOUR MOJO

ABOUT THE AUTHOR

Katandra Jackson Nunnally is the CEO of FreedomInk Publishing. She spends her time delicately balancing the role of that responsibility alongside the continuous pursuit of being an Author.

The CEO/Author resides in South East Georgia, where she shares a home with her children Jermaine Trevon, Kailyn Elise & Ashley Vanique, two pups, Liberty Rebel & Boss, and her brand new husband, Jeremy!

Formerly Katandra Shanel Jackson, Katandra Jackson Nunnally is an avid Reader, Tweeter, novice Instagramer, who's

totally obsessed with Facebook, Amazon-Ebay-Etsy peruser, a pretty darn good Chef, chauffeur, Referee, stiletto addict, Poet, Blogger, Mojo Replenisher! Did you get all of that?

Connect with 'Kat' at FreedomInk.
www.freedomink365.com/about_the_publisher

Check out these amazing books by the Author!

The Bride Diaries (The Diary of A Bride To Be Books 1, 2 & 3) is the literary romantic comedy about one girl's determination to earn the bling, wear the white dress and walk down that ever elusive aisle. Hell bent she is on claiming her version of heaven on earth. Wedded bliss will be hers even if she has to sneak up on it unsuspecting from the shadows of like, lust, love, bop it over the head, stun it into silence and carry it off, too dazed to resist, to the land of Happily Ever After! The series is funny, quirky, zany, happy, sad, full of triumphs and life's little upsets. Ladies, are you subscribed to The Bride Diaries? Guys this book is for you too! Books available at Amazon, Barnes and Noble, Books-A-Million, wherever amazing books are sold.

Be on the lookout for what's NEXT365 at FreedomInk!

Carnal Sobriety…

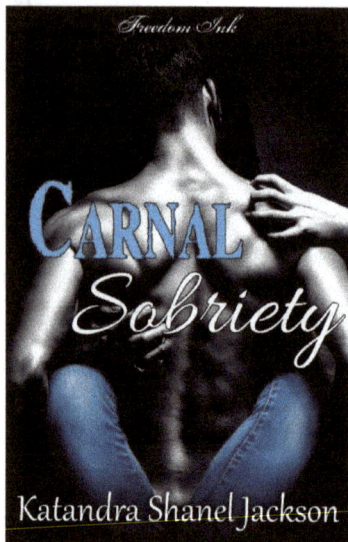

Monday through Friday. Weekends. Yes Saturdays and Sundays too. No day was holy. Sex became my religion. I sacrificed my soul for those Earth shattering minutes. Every day I locked myself away from the world. My goal? An orgasm at any cost. My vibrator was my best friend. It knew what I needed. It was what I needed. My dependency grew so strong that it became near impossible to reach climax with a temporary lover...

FreedomInk Publishing. Books that entertain, educate, embolden, empower & enlighten…

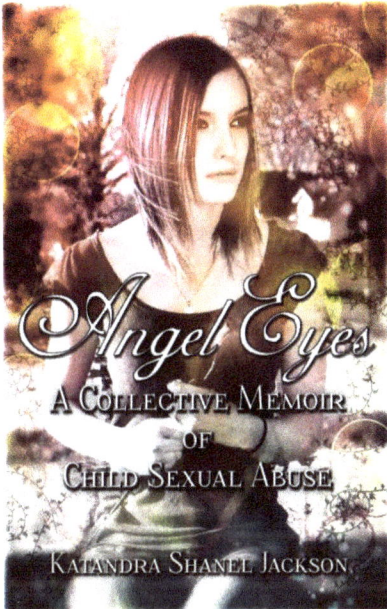

"Angel Eyes: A Collective Memoir of Child Sexual Abuse, rips open and tears down the veil of child sexual abuse, revealing the rawness of this crime against the innocent. This is not a book for the weak at heart… As you will definitely cry, and at the very least be affected. It is a book that everyone should read none-the-less, because when a people are ignorant and have a lack of understanding, we will perish and we allow this preventable disease to corrupt and grow, being passed down to our next generation..."

~Yvette Porter Moore (San Diego, California) CEO at Footprint Expressions Publishing

*This book, as well as every book published by FreedomInk is available wherever amazing books are sold.

Please contact the Publishers' home site for a custom dedication, autographed copy. www.freedomink365.com/the_books

Or contact the CEO/Author directly at katandra@freedomink365.com

Or purchase direct via this link... http://bit.ly/1pb6BoZ

We live in a world where the most debased form of humanity is applauded, shared, tweeted and reposted while the things that build us up are sometimes pushed to the background. No wonder there is so much apathy and indifference surrounding us!

Thankfully there are glimmers of hope in individuals we meet that are committed to bringing forth the best of themselves and others. Author and Publisher, Katandra Jackson Nunnally, is one of those individuals, and in the book MOJO FOR SALE we are able to take a part of what has worked for her and apply it to our own slice of the world. This book is not just about what you can do. It's about why you should want to do it. Whether she was addressing family, colleagues or things going on around us, Katandra reminds us that at the end of the day we have to be willing to realize that we are deserving of the best and that should be the attitude we take towards those we allow in our circle. If someone doesn't fit the puzzle of your life you have to be willing to discard those pieces in order to enjoy the completeness that is available to you.

For me----as with Katandra----this means recognizing that our Heavenly Father created us with greatness in our DNA and we should never allow anyone to take that away from us. This also means that we have to be so careful what we take in and what we give off, realizing how interconnected we are with each other.

After you read her thoughts, Katandra invites you to share your own, making the journey a personal one and holding yourself accountable when it comes to your happiness and peace.

Definitely a book that is entering the world at a time when it is needed the most, MOJO FOR SALE by Katandra Jackson Nunnally offers you the keys to your freedom and the opportunity to realize your own endless possibilities.

~Cyrus A. Webb, Conversations Magazine

www.ingramcontent.com/pod-product-compliance
Lightning Source LLC
Chambersburg PA
CBHW050949030426
42339CB00007B/348